They

Saw

the

Star

THEY

SAW

ADVENT
MEDITATIONS
ON
HEAVEN'S
GREATEST
GIFT

THE

STAR

JIM
WILCOX

Beacon Hill Press of Kansas City
Kansas City, Missouri

Copyright 2001
by Beacon Hill Press of Kansas City

ISBN 083-411-9145

Printed in the
United States of America

Cover Design: Kevin Williamson

Library of Congress Cataloging-in-Publication Data

Wilcox, Jim, 1952-
   They saw the star : advent meditations on heaven's greatest
gift / Jim Wilcox.
      p. cm.
   ISBN 0-8341-1914-5 (pbk.)
   1. Jesus Christ—Nativity—Meditations. 2. Christmas—Meditations. I. Title.

 BT315.2 .W492 2001
 232.92—dc21

                                          2001035816

10   9   8   7   6   5   4   3   2   1

To Linda,
who makes every day
seem like Christmas

Contents

The Star

The Escape

INTRODUCTION

No story is more familiar to the world than the story of Jesus' birth, the coming of the promised Messiah. The Word became flesh—"God with us."

Figures such as the wise men, the shepherds, the innkeeper, Herod, Joseph, and Mary are as much a part of our cultural fabric as any characters from any story ever written—or lived.

This book opens the lines of that great tale so we may see with new eyes not only the people who raised, worked beside, and followed the Christ child, but some of the difficulties they faced and the emotions they expressed. From Christ's conception to the family's escape into Egypt, Scripture is full of ideas and ideals, faults and falls, miracles and mysteries that retain profound truth for all of us, even 2,000 years later.

Many of the readings in this book spring from the story of Immanuel's birth, words that come directly from the lines of Matthew's account, comprising the first two chapters of that book. As you read, allow your imagination to capture the moment of epiphany: "Behold!"

The Facts

Matt. 1:18-19

These are the facts concerning the birth of Jesus Christ: His mother, Mary, was engaged to be married to Joseph. But while she was still a virgin she became pregnant by the Holy Spirit. Then Joseph, her fiancé, being a man of stern principle, decided to break the engagement but to do it quietly, as he didn't want to publicly disgrace her (TLB).

BIRTH

The birth of a child today is not only a "blessed event," but also huge industry. From prenatal classes and medical care to postnatal counseling and childcare, this most natural of human instincts is worth billions of dollars.

That's what makes Christ's birth, perhaps, seem even more incredible. Modern medicine, transportation, and accommodations provide as much comfort as is humanly possible to a mother in the throes of labor these days. But Mary, the mother of God's Son, had to travel by camel and mule for several days before giving birth; probably bit down on reeds during hours of unassisted, unmedicated labor; and as if that weren't enough, shared birthing quarters with cattle and their dung, flies, and disease.

The floor of the stable was most likely dirt, covered with a thin layer of hay and hay dust. The water used to wash the Newborn, therefore, might have been polluted, and the swaddling clothes might have been washed in that same water. Insects carrying life-threatening diseases might have crawled and flown all around the new mother and Child.

Imagine, if you can, a small woman at the end of a nine-month pregnancy, ostracized by her community, possibly running in utter fear for her own life (after all, according to the Old Testament law, she technically could have been stoned for fornication since she was unmarried and pregnant—although at that point in history the Jews weren't allowed to stone people), riding on the back of a farm animal day and night, finding only a semblance of shelter behind a small inn, lying on a bug-infested dirt floor, giving birth at a time when nine out of ten infants died.

And we call that Child "blessed Messiah."

Mary

The mother of Jesus is the most famous mother in the world, but that's not what makes her unique. What makes her unique is the fact that she conceived by the Holy Spirit and months later gave birth to God's only Son.

As extraordinary as that fact is, however, Christmas seems an appropriate season to celebrate the estate of motherhood and honor all mothers everywhere. After all, every one of us has a mother, so why should we wait until Mother's Day to tell her how much she means to us?

From the day we enter this world, screaming and flailing about as if we own the joint, our mothers love us unconditionally. Despite all our efforts and all our selfishness, nothing can ever change that.

When we were in trouble or felt threatened as small children, it wasn't Daddy's name we screamed as we ran toward home—it was "Mommy! Mommy! Mommy!"

When our mothers gave us chores to do before we went outside to play, they were preparing us for the real world of "work first—play later."

When our mothers disciplined us for staying out too late, it wasn't that they wanted to be mean. On the contrary, they were simply reminding us that a big chunk of their heart was missing until we came back home.

When we ate stacks of pancakes after a great night's sleep or dined on steaks and salads after a full day at school, that food didn't just drop from the sky. Mom spent a good part of her day shopping, buying, cooking, and presenting it. She loved to see us well nourished.

And even after we've grown up and flown the nest, our Mom's spirit still tucks us in our beds at night and whispers, "Sweet dreams, child."

To put it simply—when a man gives his life for a cause greater than himself, society calls him a "martyr." But when a woman gives her life for a cause greater than herself, we call her "mother."

JOSEPH

The adoptive earthly father of the Christ child must have thought he was having a bad day—more likely a *series* of bad days.

On one day he learned the girl he was planning to marry had become pregnant; another day, he was dreaming the weirdest hallucinations imaginable; later he was running from an angry king and building his carpentry business again in a new country.

It was just a string of bad luck. At least that must have entered his mind a time or two—don't you think? He was human, after all.

Even on its best days, fatherhood is challenging if not downright frightening. "Did I do the right thing?" "Should I have made her do that?" "Am I letting him get by with too much?" "Oh, why did I have kids in the first place?"

I think a father could do much worse than trying to teach his children the following lessons I've tried to teach to mine:

Don't take yourself, your successes or your failures, too seriously. To remain spiritually balanced and psychologically healthy, deflect the praise and reflect on the blame. Earn your success and learn from your failure, but never ever be afraid to fail.

Failure is the salt that flavors success. One

can never truly know the thrill of being on the mountaintop if he or she can't recall the despair of falling into the pits. Tony Campolo writes in his book *Who Switched the Price Tags?* about a number of elderly persons who responded to the question "What would you do differently if you could go back and relive your lives?" One of the dominating answers was "I would risk more." These people had learned the value of failure.

Intelligence is measured less by the ability to answer the questions than it is by the agility to ask them. Anyone can figure out the answer, given enough time or resources. But the impressive minds who have impacted the world with their passions and zeal are the curious minds who never stop asking questions.

Don't believe everything you read or hear—but with all your heart believe everything you write or say. The world is full of lies and deceptions, but if you want to become a man or woman of integrity, you must have conviction about the words of your mouth and the meditation of your heart.

Look at the big picture. When facing decisions, ask yourself, "If this were my last day on earth, would I do what I'm considering?" "Will any of this matter in 30 years? 30 days? 30 minutes?" "Is this really how I want to be remembered?"

Love your job. Don't waste 40 years of your life in a career you don't love simply because it provides security and salary. If you can't wait to get there most days, change jobs.

DREAMS

Mary and Joseph dreamed of the Holy Spirit's leading them to safety and prosperity as the parents of the Christ child.

Most of us have dreams, too, but if you're like me, I'm not sure I could call my dreams of flying through my house and over rooftops, or saving my family from a group of terrorists, inspired by the Holy Spirit.

When I was a child, I dreamed of becoming a fireman like my Uncle Carl, or a policeman like the man who lived next door to my grandparents, or an ambulance driver like the guys I saw on television. In fact, I remember spending an entire rainy Saturday sitting in front of a mirror and drawing myself in those three uniforms. (I daydreamed a lot when I was young. I'm afraid I still do.)

Funny thing was, even *after* I grew up, I still had dreams of what I wanted to be when I "grew up."

When I was about 24, I had been in school for 19 straight years but was still clueless about where I wanted to make my mark in this life. My roommate's brother, Lonnie, rescued me from my depression one afternoon by asking me, "What three things would you *love to do* in life? Just dream."

And this is what I wrote down that afternoon: "Be a professional comedian, a rock-and-roll singer, the editor of a small-town weekly newspaper." Rather diverse, I admit, but I had no idea that I served a God of diversity.

Now, a quarter of a century later, I'm a journalism professor who has up to five captive audiences a day for my demented sense of humor. I've been on stage many times during our school's variety shows singing rock and roll. And as part of my teaching, I'm the adviser and columnist for our campus' weekly newspaper.

So I tell anyone who's reading: *be careful of what you dream.*

INTEGRITY

"No, I've been awake for hours."

"Yes, I'll call you."

"The check is in the mail."

"Sure—I can claim all magazine subscriptions as a business expense."

Do times in life exist when not telling the truth is better than telling it? Do situations happen in which tact and truth seem to butt heads? Is there a difference between fibbing and lying? Between "little white lies" and "big whoppers"?

Old people don't seem to be bothered by these dilemmas as much as we younger folks are. Walk into Grandma's house with a pierced ear or a tattoo, and she's likely to blurt out in all sincerity, "No, I don't like that at all," or worse—"Not in my house you don't."

Small children are pretty honest too. Louise stopped singing to her babies at night many years ago when the younger one recoiled and said, "Bad breath, Mommy!" Several more years would pass before the little guy learned the subtlety of tact.

Joseph was a man of integrity, what the *New International Version* calls "a righteous man" and *The Living Bible* calls "a man of stern principle." He followed through with his commitments and stayed true to his word. He didn't hedge the truth or hide from it. His courage was in the promises of the Lord.

Wouldn't be an interesting place to live if being truthful were the *norm?* It would certainly take some getting used to, no doubt about that, but wouldn't it also be quite refreshing to know that nobody is lying to you or lying to others about you?

During a Christmas break a few years ago, one of my students went to eat at a local restaurant with several friends. When the bill came, he noticed that the server had undercharged him by more than $8.

Travis (not his real name) showed the bill to his friends, and they began to laugh at the mistake and reason that this was just his good fortune. He even told his friends that it was God's way of reimbursing him for our school's high tuition.

Imagine those young people's reaction if the bill had been an *over*charge of $8. Do you think they would have taken that as "a sign from God"?

Integrity is being honest and accountable even when nobody is watching. Who knows what might have happened to Mary—young, unmarried, and pregnant—if Joseph had not been a righteous man of stern principle!

MARRIAGE

If you want to give your spouse the perfect Christmas present this year, cut this page out, put it in a new frame, and put it on his or her pillow on Christmas Eve.

These are ten wedding vows that are rarely actually spoken at weddings but should be repeated frequently after that day to keep the marriage strong.

1. I shall be creative and imaginative when thinking of ways to surprise you. That's how I shall keep the romance of our early days alive and kicking into our twilight years.

2. I shall remember all the little anniversaries with a card or a gift: the first date, the first time we held hands, the first kiss, the first time I said, "I love you," the day we became engaged, and others.

3. I shall put the toilet seat and "doughnut" down *and* flush after every use.

4. I shall leave the tedium of my work at the office and bring home only the burdens I must share or the joys I want to celebrate.

5. I shall be careful with our finances without being miserly, and generous without being irresponsible.

6. I shall not "keep score" of past transgressions to bring up later when our emotions are fragile and volatile. Once forgiven, the past shall be forgotten.

7. I shall listen with both ears and both eyes—but neither lip.

8. I shall grow old worshiping the Lord with you.

9. I shall learn to run the clothes washer, the dishwasher, the vacuum cleaner, and the lawn mower.

10. I shall not reserve "please" and "thank you" and "excuse me" for perfect strangers or mere acquaintances.

THE SPIRIT OF CHRISTMAS

The day was one of those blustery winter days that many of us love: overcast and cold with something in the air between snow and ice. This was a jacket-and-sweater day, a prelude to Christmas.

Every Tuesday for a couple of years, I took college students to lunch—as many as showed up to my office with a little bit of time and cash on their hands. We would spend an hour joking, laughing, and just enjoying being together, trying to break the monotony of tests, papers, and class notes. Frankly, I needed it as much as they did.

On this particular Tuesday only Brad and Kyle showed up. Kyle was a student leader who is now a medical doctor doing great things for the Kingdom in Texas. We had one of those strange relationships that looked childish but felt much deeper. In a nutshell, Kyle used to kick me all the time—at church, at school, at my home. Instead of shaking my hand when offered, he would kick me in the shins. I always thought it was weird, but he seemed to enjoy it immensely.

Brad, on the other hand, was quiet and unassuming, but he had a heart of gold and the heart of God. He was very handsome and very sensitive to the Holy Spirit, but he was so kind to me I couldn't be jealous.

So on this Tuesday, Brad, Kyle, and I piled into my Buick Century and slid downtown to the City Rescue Mission, where we were to have lunch and spend part of the afternoon stuffing flyers into envelopes. We had our broth and buttered bread with the other men of the mission and then began our work.

When it neared 3:00, I knew the guys needed to get back to campus, so we headed toward the door, but Brad lagged behind a bit. Kyle and I fetched the car and waited outside in the sleet and snow for Brad, and soon he bounded out the door in only an undershirt.

When he got in the car, I asked, "Hey—where's that beautiful jacket and new sweater you had on when we got here?"

With no trumpets or fanfare to pronounce it, Brad said in his simple and humble way, "Oh, there was some guy in there who was freezing, so I gave them to him. Can we go now?"

The spirit of Christmas was shown to me that day in a way I'll never forget—someone in need and someone who could fill that need. I want my life to reflect that kind of giving. Don't you?

MANHOOD

Men buy their wives or girlfriends thoughtful, romantic gifts at Christmas.

Boys buy them things that plug into a wall socket or the car lighter.

Men know that presentation of the gift is half the fun.

Boys just throw the thing into a bag.

Men wear flannel shirts and tromp into a field to cut down the perfect Christmas tree.

Boys are content with three lights, five ornaments, and a tree from a kit.

Men sit near their stereos listening to Andy Williams sing Christmas carols.

Boys stand in front of cute girls' front doors, singing off-key Christmas carols.

Men like to give at Christmas.

Boys like to get.

Men spend their time and resources trying to make the world a better place.

Boys spend their time and resources trying to fill the void with better toys.

Men know where they're taking their dates and how much money it will cost.

Boys get into the car and whine, "Where you wanna go? Hey—you got cash?"

Men drive the speed limit, use their turn signals, and call the officer "Sir."

Boys squeal their tires around corners at 60 and call their cars "Maria."

Men curb their behavior based on the integrity and history of their last name.

Boys base their behavior on instant self-gratification.

Men look at life through a telescope and see the important and imperative.

Boys look at life through a microscope and see the immediate and improbable.

Men know that it takes strength of character to become humble and forgiving.

Boys see meekness as only a sign of weakness.

MEN DON'T ASK

A silly point of pride among men is that they'll always know where they are when they're behind the wheel of a car. Put them at the helm on a road trip from one Christmas in-law's to another, and they would sooner die than stop to ask for directions—or consult a road map.

I have a friend who once passed the same gas station five times before we could convince him that he had spent the last hour driving in circles around Dallas. He truly thought that every Christmas tree lot we passed was plopped between a Denny's and a freeway ramp to Houston.

Perhaps the stupidest case of directional dyslexia happened to my brother and me when we went for a leisurely stroll in Juneau, Alaska. Both being men—stubborn men, stubborn Wilcox men—each of us was determined to lead, and that can mean only one thing: utter confusion.

When we got to the intersection of our hosts' neighborhood with the main road to town, John absolutely knew we should go right. I, on the other hand, had the gift of navigational genius and knew with the certainty of a guiding star in the heavens that we should go left.

So there we stood, miles from where we wanted to be, trying to decide if our next step should be to the right—or to the left. Never mind that there were houses and people about. This decision was a test of our manhood (such as it is).

First we went to the right (he's bigger than I am), but after 100 yards, we agreed that we had made a mistake. So we went back to the intersection and walked maybe 200 yards in the other direction. But then things didn't look right there, either, so we turned around and walked the 200 yards back to the intersection.

Anybody with half a mind would have knocked on a door, but the Wilcox twins don't knock on doors (unless they're Christmas caroling for money in July).

Off we went again to the right, this time about 300 yards from our point of origin. But once again the scenery seemed baffling and strange, so we once again walked the 300 yards back to the intersection.

This is a true story. One more time we tried the left route and got about 400 yards before we gave up. By this time we had walked what seemed like 10 miles and were literally right where we had started. John was so exasperated and fatigued ("My loins are on fire!" he screamed) that he trudged back to our hosts' house and took a nap, leaving me to my own devices.

Eventually I made it to the fat-free yogurt shop in downtown Juneau and treated myself to an extra-large.

I guess God knew better than to waste a huge bright star on two stubborn men.

RIGHTEOUSNESS VS. PUBLIC DISGRACE

Love and faithfulness are really the "heads and tails" of the same coin, aren't they? When you stop and think about it, it's utterly impossible to love someone without being faithful to him or her.

That means that even if the person lies about you in a rumor that circulates through your entire circle of family and friends, you refrain from retaliation. Being the victim of a rumor should, instead, cure you from ever being a part of another one.

That means that if he or she borrows your favorite sweater without asking first, then ruins it, you recognize that the value of your friendship is worth far more than that pullover.

That means that when you promise in front of everyone you cherish that you'll love this person until the day you die, you rise every morning of your life with his or her happiness and well-being as your sole purpose.

That means that if his or her schedule makes you feel neglected, you ask in all sincerity how you might help relieve some of the stress so that he or she might find time to relax.

That means that you pour yourself into the lives of your children, being certain to attend each game, each performance, each recital, each program with enthusiasm.

That means that you don't just sit around to answer the bell, but that you actually go out and seek opportunities to serve the ones you love: you send them a card, mow their yard, cook them dinner, wash their car, clean their house, help them study.

That means you never embarrass them in public, never ridicule them in private, never discourage or disparage them.

Matthew tells us that "Joseph her husband was a righteous man and did not want to expose [Mary] to public disgrace" (Matt. 1:19). Let this be a reminder this Christmas season to love one another with righteousness, seeking the good of the other more than seeking good for ourselves.

The gift of love is surely the greatest gift of all.

The Dream

Matt. 1:20-21

As he lay awake considering this, he fell into a dream, and saw an angel standing beside him. "Joseph, son of David," the angel said, "don't hesitate to take Mary as your wife! For the child within her has been conceived by the Holy Spirit. And she will have a Son, and you shall name Him Jesus (meaning 'Savior'), for he will save his people from their sins" (TLB).

THINKING

The simple act of thinking has become a luxury in our culture. We're far too rushed and important and involved to have time to sit in our favorite chair, staring out our favorite window, pondering the world and the universe. Or creating. Or inventing.

Michele McCormick wrote an essay for *Newsweek* a few years ago (March 29, 1993, 10) titled "We're Too Busy for Ideas." She uses the metaphor of the Walkman, the portable radio-headphone set, to suggest that when she became fully "plugged in," things stopped occurring to her. She writes:

> The old story has it that Isaac Newton identified the concept and presence of gravity while sitting under an apple tree. One fruit fell and science gained a new dimension.
>
> While there may be some historic license in that tale, it's easy to see that if Newton had been wearing his Walkman, he probably would have overlooked the real impact of the apple's fall.

Our culture has made information the almighty currency of power, and we can't have the power unless we're plugged in 24/7/365, as they say. As a result, things have stopped occurring to us.

Unlike ancient Israel and Greece and Rome, we don't pay much attention to wisdom, the by-prod-

33

uct of thinking, and we certainly don't reward it. If we did, old people would be among the richest segment of our society rather than the poorest.

In his book *Who Switched the Price Tags?* cited earlier, Tony Campolo gives another dominant response of a group of elderly persons to the question "What would you do differently if you could go back and relive your lives?" Many said, "I would take time to reflect more." One man put it this way: "I would take more baths and fewer showers." In other words, these people would think, ponder, meditate, create, and invent more. And they would have hurried, pushed, driven, and dashed around much less.

At this Christmas season, thinking might be the best gift you could give yourself. Take a few hours in your favorite chair next to your favorite window with a cup of coffee, a piece of pecan pie, staring, thinking, and . . .

DESCENDANTS

Former talk-show-host-turned-rich-recluse Johnny Carson used to joke every Christmas that, in fact, only one fruitcake exists in the world. It simply gets passed around from family to family, from country to country, from century to century.

I must admit I've never seen anybody actually eat a fruitcake. Have you? I mean, who would? Who *could?*

I recently looked up the ingredients of a fruitcake in my wife's cookbook: "Candied cherries, snipped dates, candied pineapple, candied fruit peeling, molasses, gun powder, ground chuck, Ninja Turtle extract, and rum extract."

Uh—I think I'll pass.

Fruitcake at Christmas is really like that cranberry sauce at Thanksgiving—a lovely table garnish, but nothing human beings should actually eat. It's surely never been a staple at our house.

At our house, *fruitcake* was the label we attached to loony relatives.

"Oh, that Aunt Esther! She's as nutty as a fruitcake!" we would chuckle quietly to each other as we watched Aunt Esther through the window watering her plastic poinsettias.

"Why, just last week," her sister-in-law would announce, "she locked one of her chickens out of the hen house during a windstorm, and that bird ended up laying the same egg 12 times!"

Over the past few years, lots of people I work with and several of my students have used that sobriquet when referring to me: "That guy made us write a letter to Mark Twain in class today. Twain's been dead for a hundred years. What a fruitcake!"

So this year, when your house becomes the target for the world's only fruitcake, think of my Aunt Esther's poor chicken. Think about my poor students.

And think about having a slice of pecan pie instead.

WIFE

(Rather than writing about wives at Christmas, I asked my wife to write about Christmas. Thank you, Linda.)

By Linda Wilcox

Christmas starts for me on November 1. The fireplace is going (who cares if we sometimes have to put on shorts?), I'm singing "Blue Christmas" along with Elvis, and we're all in the attic digging for Christmas ornaments.

Most of the Christmas ornaments that make it from the tree back to our attic year after year were made by tiny hands in Sunday School or kindergarten, or bought at the annual January 75-per-cent-off sale that Walgreen's holds.

But there's another kind of ornament I think about throughout the year—the people who have adorned my life and decorated my walk with God.

Like my Granny Patterson, a tiny bird-like woman who until her death at 88 was one of the most outspoken people I have ever known. She said and did just about whatever she pleased in her later life. And stubborn? Who else leaves her clocks at the same time year-round just because she doesn't see the point of daylight saving time?

Surprisingly, however, she had a network of friends I couldn't believe. They were usually drawn to her because of her honesty. It became the ornament she left me when she died.

A professor during my junior year of college made us all a little uncomfortable by challenging us to be "thinking Christians." He frequently asked us to climb out of our middle-class comfort zones and care about the poor around us. It's safe to say that I chose my career in sociology because of Jerry Hull's example of compassion. What a great ornament he gave me!

Finally there's my friend Sharon. We think alike on almost everything important—including our common love of anything chocolate. She has moved away from our area, but her loyalty remains one ornament I treasure to this day.

I hope I can be more like these "ornaments" of Christlikeness who have adorned my life.

Son

Sometimes we forget that only sons were honored in the family during Biblical times. Only sons received inheritances. Only sons bore the name of the father.

In most industrialized nations today, daughters are equally welcomed into the home and given equal rights under the law. That must be a huge comfort to Roy Kettelhut and Mike Brooks, two friends of mine who have three daughters and no sons.

I wonder what happened to the Roys and Mikes of ancient Galilee—their daughters, their wealth, their bloodlines. Did society act as if they had never existed?

God has blessed my wife and me with two great sons: Benjamin and Joshua. If Ben had been born in first-century Judea, we might have called him "Ben ben James," which would have meant, "Ben, son of James." According to most etymologists, however, Benjamin means "son of the right hand," which is fine with me since I'm right-handed.

Joshua, also a name from the Old Testament, is the Hebrew version of "Jesus," which we learn in Matthew's account means "Savior." We'll see if there's any significance to his name as he grows older.

Ben has inherited his father's curse of curiosity.

39

I suppose sometimes curiosity is a good thing, but for Ben, it's always been somewhat costly.

For instance, I recall the Christmas morning when he was about five or six that he received a Fisher-Price tape recorder to "record his world," according to his mother. We learned that afternoon, however, that Ben's world was more about *how* things are recorded rather than the things themselves.

We found him at about 3:00, in the middle of the garage floor, with his dad's tools all around him and parts of the brand-new tape recorder spread from one wall to the other. "I just wanted to know where the sound went," he explained with a groan.

Josh has done none of that—mostly because Ben had lost nearly every one of my tools years before. But no human on the face of God's green earth is pickier about what he wears than our Joshua.

I mean to tell you, if he didn't pick it out of an expensive Christmas catalog that arrived among the annual Christmas letters from people we haven't thought about since last Christmas, that red shirt or green sweater or blue jacket, thoughtfully purchased and carefully wrapped, will never see the light of day on his back.

After all, he has an "image" to uphold.

Yeah, well I did, too. Until I had my two little lambs.

Jesus

Jesus of Nazareth is the only God-man ever to have lived. He was 100 percent God and 100 percent man, the only 200-percent being ever born.

What does this mean to us?

First it means He understands us. He knows how we're tempted from every side, for He, too, was tempted. Matt. 4:1-11 tells us that He was led into the desert for 40 days, during which he was visited by Satan, who tempted Him to give up His mission and follow the ways of the flesh.

Jesus, the human being, also knows how we're discouraged, despondent, and depressed, for He, too, was discouraged. In looking over Jerusalem, the Holy City, He said, "O Jerusalem, Jerusalem, you who kill the prophets and stone those sent to you, how often I have longed to gather your children together, as a hen gathers her chicks under her wings, but you were not willing. Look, your house is left to you desolate" (Matt. 23:37-38).

Jesus the human being also knows how we're deserted and ignored. When He prayed in the garden alone, His disciples slept instead of remaining prayerfully vigilant. When he was arrested, His "Rock," Peter, disgraced Him with denial three times. Even on the Cross, He asked His Heavenly Father why He had been forsaken.

But Jesus the Son of God was also divine. That means He is omnipresent—everywhere. The writer of Ps. 139 expresses it this way: "If I go up to the heavens, you are there; if I make my bed in the depths, you are there. If I rise on the wings of the dawn, if I settle on the far side of the sea, even there your hand will guide me, your right hand will hold me fast" (vv. 8-10).

Jesus, the Son of God, is also omniscient, all-knowing. Again in Ps. 139, the psalmist sings, "O LORD, you have searched me and you know me. You know when I sit and when I rise; you perceive my thoughts from afar. You discern my going out and my lying down; you are familiar with all my ways. Before a word is on my tongue you know it completely, O LORD" (vv. 1-4).

Jesus, the Son of God, is also omnipotent, all-powerful. From Ps. 139 again: "You created my inmost being; you knit me together in my mother's womb. I praise you because I am fearfully and wonderfully made; your works are wonderful, I know that full well" (vv. 13-14).

"And he will be called Wonderful Counselor, Mighty God, Everlasting Father, Prince of Peace" (Isa. 9:6).

SALVATION

Christ came to Earth for one reason: to reconcile God to humanity, and humanity to God. To renew the covenant. To make amends.

His birth we celebrate this season is only the beginning of His mission. He came in the form of a baby so that we might have life and have it abundantly. But that abundant life is possible only through His sacrificial death on the Cross and His glorious resurrection from the grave.

Praise the Lord for His birth, but without Good Friday and Resurrection Sunday, it would have been only that: a birth. Forgiveness would have been impossible. Human beings are not capable of complete and utter forgiveness. Not on their own, they're not.

Only the mercy and grace of the Holy Spirit dwelling in the heart of a Christian allows him or her to participate in the divine plan of forgiveness.

Saying, "I'm sorry," "Apology accepted," or even "I forgive you" is only the beginning, but absolute forgiveness goes into the realm of forgetting the wrong. And forgetting others' transgressions is not human nature.

No matter how much we want to forget another's breach of trust, 100-percent trust can never be restored. Only the plenary infusion of the Holy Spirit can do that.

What Christ asked His Father to do, then, when

He said, "Father, forgive them, for they do not know what they are doing" (Matt. 23:34) is inconceivable to us. We can read it over and over again, brothers and sisters, but forgiving His own executioners for His wrongful death is not human. Forgetting it is not human. You and I are incapable of such an act of holiness.

After all, has humanity forgotten the Crucifixion over the past 2,000 years? Has humanity forgiven Caesar's soldiers?

Father, forgive me, for I do not know what I am doing.

Sin

When I was about 10 years old, my parents took us kids on long trips every summer. We would load the Chevrolet station wagon and head out to see parts of North America that only magazines had revealed to us.

One such journey took us to Carlsbad Caverns National Park of New Mexico, where every evening at precisely the same moment, millions of bats soar like eerie black clouds out of the caverns' mouth and into the evening sky to feed on nocturnal insects. (That could literally drive a person batty if he or she scares easily.)

The next morning our family went on a guided hike into the depths of the caverns, often sighting fuzzy carpets of dozing bats on the cave's ceilings and remembering the night before.

When we got to the deepest part of the cave, the guide told everybody to grab hold of something or somebody because he was about to turn out the lights.

I was certain I would still be able to see, but when the cave was darkened, was I glad to be within an arm's reach of my parents. It was absolutely black. I put my hand in front of my face and saw nothing. "Maybe my eyes aren't even open," I thought, but when I checked by poking my eye rather painfully, I found my eyes were bugged out of their sockets. Still I saw nothing!

Then the guide's flashlight came on, followed by the entire cave's lighting system. Immediately we were back in a lighted cave and were soon outside, where the summer sun shone painfully brightly.

From absolute dark to absolute light—like righteousness to the sinner.

Many people you know this Christmas are in the absolute black darkness of sin, unable to see the path, unwilling to take that first frightening step.

When the Christ child of Christmas grew up to be a man, He admonished each of His followers to be "the light of the world. . . . Let your light shine before men, that they may see your good deeds and praise your Father in heaven" (Matt. 5:14, 16).

Don't hide your lamp under a bowl. Take it into the darkness and bring the light to a frightened soul.

THE PROPHECY

Matt. 1:22—2:2

"This will fulfill God's message through His prophets—

'Listen! The virgin shall conceive a child! She shall give birth to a Son, and He shall be called "Emmanuel" (meaning "God is with us").'"

When Joseph awoke, he did as the angel commanded, and brought Mary home to be his wife, but she remained a virgin until her Son was born; and Joseph named Him "Jesus."

Jesus was born in the town of Bethlehem, in Judea, during the reign of King Herod. At about that time some astrologers from eastern lands arrived in Jerusalem, asking, "Where is the newborn King of the Jews? For we have seen His star in far-off eastern lands, and have come to worship Him" (TLB).

PROPHECY

When Jack was an adventurous tyke, he spent many summer days studying the lives of insects. He discovered the answer to the question "What makes bees sting?" one blistering afternoon when he slapped one too many bees in his front yard's clover.

But in order to find out what made some butterflies' wings so colorful, Jack had to catch one, and that demanded a jar from his mom's supply of canning jars in the garage. Unfortunately, the empty ones were on the top shelf, so he had to climb up and up and up. With the perfect jar in hand, however, Jack fell to the floor of the garage, cutting his hand badly.

Jack's mom rushed him to the local hospital's emergency room, where he was placed on the other side of the curtain from a man who had just cut off his leg with a chainsaw. The frantic doctors had little time to spend on a seven-year-old's cut finger, so instead of anesthetizing him before stitching, they simply started sewing him up.

As you might imagine, it hurts to have a needle go through your skin, followed by the pulling of a long string, so Jack screamed in torturous pain. He couldn't help it, even though the doctors told him he was disturbing the man next door.

So in order to quiet Jack, the attending nurse poured water down his throat to stop the screaming. It was highly effective, but it scared poor Jack even more.

Upon hearing Jack's tale, his mom nearly dismantled the emergency room single-handedly, anxious to let the staff know that her son would never again be treated at that establishment.

And Jack learned that day that when Mom and Dad told him not to climb up the garage shelves, they had a good reason.

You see, moms and dads seem to have the gift of prophecy, and they know that one thing will indeed lead to another. They know that some risks are just not worth taking. They know that every decision carries with it a consequence.

Like God, they have the experience to know what will probably happen. And like angels, they send warnings and good tidings ahead of time.

And only when a child like Jack becomes a parent himself will he begin to understand that mystery of mysteries.

BETHLEHEM

O little town of Bethlehem,
How still we see thee lie!
Bethlehem was the Hebrew word meaning
"house of bread" and had been the home of both
Ruth and King David, when it was called
Ephratah. It was a town located about six miles
south of Jerusalem, the Holy City, and about 70
miles south of Nazareth, the home of Christ during
His childhood.

It was not uncommon for a person's world and
experience to be limited to a region within a 10-
mile radius of his or her home. That's hard to
imagine in today's world of supersonic jets, satel-
lites and telephones.

Above thy deep and dreamless sleep
The silent stars go by.
December 25 was probably not the actual birth
date of the Messiah. Winter was wet and cold in
that part of the world, so shepherds were probably
not out in the harsh elements tending sheep. It is
much more likely that Jesus was born in the
spring, when lambs were born and the skies were
clear and the nights were fairly mild.

The date for Christmas was chosen in the
fourth century as a direct assault on the pagan
holiday known as "Natalis Invicti," a holiday infa-

mous for its ribald and raucous behavior. By celebrating Christ's coming on that day, Christians had a purer reason to join the secular celebrating.

> *Yet in thy dark streets shineth*
> *The everlasting Light;*

Jews all over Israel were returning to the cities of their ancestors to report for the census that led to Roman taxing, but Joseph and Mary, who had traveled many hours on muleback, could find no place to stay. The stable we see in our celebrations today was probably a cave in which livestock was kept.

Jesus' location was revealed by a bright star, and the angels heralded his birth with glorious singing. John says in his gospel, "In him was life, and that life was the light of men. The light shines in the darkness, but the darkness has not understood it" (John 1:4-5).

> *The hopes and fears of all the years*
> *Are met in thee tonight.*

Jews the world over had been awaiting the coming of the Christ, the King of Israel, for centuries. He was to be their deliverance from the terror and horror of Caesar and the Roman Empire. In Him they placed their hopes of living in freedom and justice as God's chosen nation.

Isn't it tragic that most of His own people failed to recognize Him? Let's praise Him this season for revealing himself to each of us individually, for He brings "good news of great joy" (Luke 2:10).

HEROD

"King Herod the Great." No four words brought more fear into the hearts of Judeans.

Herod—the man who had drowned his brother-in-law, executed his uncle, and framed Hyrcanus II for getting in his way. Herod—the man who was manic-depressive and had violent mood swings. Herod—the man who on a whim or fancy would order the murder of friend or foe or family. Herod—the man who executed his favorite wife and then had the audacity to mourn her death publicly.

Herod was a man at the top, at the top of paranoia and iron-fisted rule. He broke any and every Jewish law, introducing Greek games and architecture to his land. He played up to Caesar Augustus and barred public gatherings when Caesar visited, fearing open revolution.

Herod's ten wives bore him many sons, most of whom would die at their father's hand when he discovered their plots to overthrow him.

No one should have been surprised when as Herod neared the end of his life at around age 70 and heard of the birth of the long-anticipated and prophesied "King of Israel," he lashed out one final time, ordering the slaughter of all male babies under the age of two.

But unlike Herod, God protected His only begotten Son, who escaped to Egypt with His earthly parents.

Jews

At the time of Jesus' birth in Bethlehem, Jews were scattered throughout the Roman Empire. So when we read that the little family of three fled to Egypt to escape Herod's wrath, it may be somewhat comforting to us—and certainly was to them—to realize that they were fleeing to a place that actually had some Jews.

Judaism is based on the Old Testament, the scriptures of Moses and the Prophets. While Jews were allowed to pray and worship God anywhere, only one place on Earth was holy enough for them to bring sacrificial offerings to. That was the Holy Temple in Jerusalem.

The Temple had been built, ironically, by Herod, the father of Herod Antipas, and was the largest, most magnificent building in the Roman Empire. It was four times the size of the Acropolis and twice as big as the forum in Rome. The compound itself covered 35 acres.

Jerusalem, a city of about 50,000 residents, was strategically placed at the center of commerce and pilgrimages. More than 100,000 Jews passed through on their way to celebrate Passover every year. It would seem logical, therefore, that Hebrew, Latin, and Greek languages were all used easily in the cosmopolitan center of culture.

The Sanhedrin was the ruling council, given its power to enforce Jewish laws by the Roman Caesar. However, Rome was never comfortable giving total jurisdiction to the Sanhedrin, and as a result, a great tension always existed between the Jews and Rome. Much of this tension was focused on Roman taxation.

This taxation set into motion Mary and Joseph's flight to nearby Bethlehem for Jesus' birth.

THE STAR

If we had only had a star to guide us out of the valley and over Big Bear Mountain.

Life is little more than a series of lessons, we'll all agree, so I should not have been surprised during Christmas 1989 to learn a lesson that would change my Christmas celebrations forever and ever. Hallelujah!

It did surprise me, though.

That was the last Christmas that my family made the trip to West Virginia by traveling over the world's most dangerous road—the one over Big Bear Mountain.

I should have known something ominous was in store for me that blustery Monday morning when our little Honda Civic slid around like a hockey puck while we were just pulling out of my in-laws' driveway to make the trip back home. When we got to the slight rise on the little road outside my in-laws' house, well, you can forget about it. We would be staying another night . . . and day . . . and night if that's what it took to feel rubber on asphalt.

Three times we backed up a line of cars behind us so we could get another running start at the "hill" until finally, with lots of screaming and coaxing and rocking, we made it up and out to the dreaded Interstate 77 just outside Beckley, West Virginia.

Ten minutes after entering that ice-covered, snow-blinded, snake-curving highway, we knew we were in trouble. Cars on our left were suddenly on our right. Vans going south were abruptly jerked north. And then, without warning, the 18-wheeler in front of us jackknifed 180 degrees and began barreling right at us.

I not only prayed to Jesus—I *saw* Him, right smack-dab in the middle of that huge truck grill coming straight at me. *Lord, I'm coming home!*

Aren't you glad that the wise men and shepherds had a navigation system for their journey, a tracking device that led them out of danger and into the sanctuary of the humble stable?

As you look into the heavens this holiday season and ponder the magnificence of God's creative universe, imagine a star so bright, a star so compelling, that you just had to pack up and follow it.

And then thank the Lord you're not on Big Bear Mountain in a driving blizzard.

I know I will.

Worship

One reason to worship the Almighty is that it puts us in our place.

Think about it. Most of us spend much of our time pushing our own agendas and tooting our own horns and doing the work that satisfies our own desires and needs. In many ways, we "worship" ourselves most of each week.

But when we bow our heads and kneel our bodies before the throne of God, the Creator and Sustainer of the Universe and all that's in it, when we prostrate ourselves at the foot of His cross, we recognize the proper order of everything.

When we worship, and perhaps *only* when we worship, we let our hearts be united with His Great Heart, pulses finding the same rhythm, purposes finding the same direction.

Christmas in North America has almost become the antithesis to worship in its purest sense. Instead of focusing our attention on the eternal and divine, we're inundated with reminders to focus on the temporal and human.

Commercials attempt to convince us that we'll not be worthy of the name "relative" if we don't buy this wonderful gift for that special someone. They preach, "Buy now—pay later." They create in us such desire that we mistake our wants for our needs.

Don't get me wrong: nothing is inherently bad

with giving gifts of the heart to the people we love. But when this comes at the cost of worshiping the Father, who gave His only Son so that we might be with Him "today . . . in paradise" (Luke 23:43), we've paid far too high a price.

This is the season in which we can make each gift under the tree a symbol of worship. Instead of concentrating on how much money we're spending to please each other, let's center our attention on gifts of the heart. His heart to ours. Our hearts to His.

JEALOUSY

King Herod was just plain jealous. He was so insecure in his man-made kingdom, and so afraid that any given day would be his last day in the throne, that when he heard of the birth of the "King of the Jews" he became unnerved.

"When King Herod heard this he was disturbed, and all Jerusalem with him. When he had called together all the people's chief priests and teachers of the law, he asked them where the Christ was to be born. . . .

"Then Herod called the Magi secretly and found out from them the exact time the star had appeared. He sent them to Bethlehem and said, 'Go and make a careful search for the child. As soon as you find him, report to me'" (Matt. 2:3-4, 7-8).

Herod's purpose, of course, was to kill this upstart rival before He had a chance to threaten his throne.

It's easy to condemn Herod because we've been privileged to know "the rest of the story," and we kind of gloat in our 20/20 hindsight. We might even be a bit proud of ourselves for knowing how wrong Herod turned out to be. After all, it's not "Herodmas" we celebrate every year.

But Christmastime is often when a lot of us, even those of us who are Christians, become a little jealous of others and threatened by their affluence, travels, extravagant gifts, beautifully decorated homes, or their 10-foot Douglas firs.

Part of the blame is our culture that pounds materialism and commercialism and consumerism into our skulls 24 hours a day. We're told countless times each day that what we have is not good enough and what the other guy has is out of our price range.

But the bulk of the blame is on our sinful nature that attempts to convince us that we deserve the best, the most expensive, the most comfortable, and the most luxurious.

Thank You, Jesus, the Babe of Bethlehem and the Christ of Calvary, for showing us that petty jealousies do nothing but destroy our spirits and that agape love feeds our hungry souls. In Your name we pray. Amen.

The Star

Matt. 2:3-11

King Herod was deeply disturbed by their question, and all Jerusalem was filled with rumors.

He called a meeting of the Jewish religious leaders. "Did the prophets tell us where the Messiah would be born?" he asked.

"Yes, in Bethlehem," they said, "for this is what the prophet Micah wrote:

'O little town of Bethlehem, you are not just an unimportant Judean village, for a Governor shall rise from you to rule my people Israel.'"

Then Herod sent a private message to the astrologers, asking them to come to see him; at this meeting he found out from them the exact time when they first saw the star. Then he told them, "Go to Bethlehem and search for the child. And when you find him, come back and tell me so that I can go and worship him too!"

After this interview the astrologers started out again. And look! The star appeared to them again, standing over Bethlehem. Their joy knew no bounds!

Entering the house where the baby and Mary his mother were, they threw themselves down before him, worshiping. Then they opened their presents and gave Him gold, frankincense and myrrh (TLB).

LAW

The birth of Christ, which we celebrate this season, marked the beginning of a new law. John records it for us in his gospel as Christ added an 11th commandment:

"A new command I give you: Love one another. As I have loved you, so you must love one another. By this all men will know that you are my disciples, if you love one another" (John 13:34-35).

The primary method we have of showing our love for each other is committing ourselves to each other. To many this is symbolized with a promise ring, engagement ring, or wedding ring. For others it's a tattoo on the arm. For most it's a friendship.

I find the combination of love and law most compelling when turning the Ten Commandments into the Ten *Commitments*.

"You are the Lord my God, who brought me out of the land of Egypt, out of the house of bondage. I shall have no other gods before you.

"I shall not make for myself a graven image, or any likeness of anything that is in heaven above, or that is in the earth beneath, or that is in the water under the earth; I shall not bow down to them or serve them; for you are a jealous God.

"I shall not take the name of the Lord my God in vain.

"I shall remember the Sabbath day, to keep it holy. Six days I shall labor, and do all my work;

but the seventh day is a Sabbath to the Lord my God.

"I shall honor my father and my mother, that my days may be long in the land which the Lord my God gives me.

"I shall not kill.

"I shall not commit adultery.

"I shall not steal.

"I shall not bear false witness.

"I shall not covet my neighbor's house, wife, workers, equipment or any material possessions he might own."

Maybe the Christmas season is the perfect time to recommit ourselves to God's law of loving Him above all else and loving each other selflessly.

Messiah

As early as the book of 2 Samuel, we read of God's promise to David that his lineage would always be on the throne of Israel. But it was the patriarch, Abraham, an ancestor of David, who began the "begats" in the Gospels that lead to Christ's birth.

This is one reason the Jews were full of disbelief when a meek Carpenter from Bethlehem claimed his rightful title as King of the Jews. He certainly did not appear to be anything like Abraham or David or Solomon.

The Jews also knew that the line of David had been interrupted—the current king was from the line of Herod.

They were looking for a deliverer who would overthrow the evil Herod in some sort of apocalyptic battle and restore rule to the anointed line of David and Solomon. ("Christ" and "Messiah" come from the Greek and Hebrew words meaning "Anointed.")

Jesus' miracles and preaching were not quite the overpowering mandate that the zealots were hoping and praying for. Even His resurrection was sign enough for only those who had followed the Master closely throughout His ministry.

Judaism today is still seeking its Messiah and chooses not to celebrate the holy day of Christmas.

But because we believe that Jesus did indeed conquer the grave and sits today at the right hand of God, we can celebrate from the depths of our hearts.

"Glory to God in the highest, and on earth peace to men on whom his favor rests. . . . I bring you good news of great joy that will be for all the people. Today in the town of David a Savior has been born to you; he is Christ the Lord. This will be a sign to you: You will find a baby wrapped in cloths and lying in a manger" (Luke 2:14, 10-12).

ISRAEL

After thousands of years and dozens of wars, after scores of plagues and persecution, the nation of Israel is still in today's headlines. Remarkable, isn't it, that the chosen people of God continue to face enemies every day?

"Israel" is the Hebrew word literally meaning "who prevails with God"—a fascinating label for a people who have had to overcome tremendous odds against them, all with the help of the Almighty, the God of Israel.

The writer of 2 Samuel writes, "All the tribes of Israel came to David at Hebron and said, 'We are your own flesh and blood. In the past, while Saul was king over us, you were the one who led Israel on their military campaigns. And the LORD said to you, "You will shepherd my people Israel, and you will become their ruler"'" (2 Sam. 5:1-2).

"The Lord's eternal love for Israel" is noted in 1 Kings 10:9. When Solomon was king, it was said, "Because of the love of your God for Israel and his desire to uphold them forever, he has made you king" (2 Chron. 9:8).

Being chosen is the greatest feeling in the world. When someone of the opposite sex *chooses* us to be his or her mate for life, we celebrate at the wedding and at every anniversary thereafter. When the captain of the second-grade baseball team *chooses* us to play with him or her, we feel like Mark McGwire and Sammy Sosa rolled into one superstar.

I've heard that adopted children feel a special bond to their parents because they were actually *chosen* to become part of their families.

God has chosen you, my friend, to be His child through the brotherhood and sisterhood with His Son, Jesus Christ. And this is the secret joy of Christmas that we celebrate.

> *So bring Him incense, gold, and myrrh;*
> *Come, peasant, king to own Him.*
> *The King of Kings salvation brings;*
> *Let loving hearts enthrone Him.*
> *This, this is Christ, the King,*
> *Whom shepherds guard and angels sing.*
> *Haste, haste, to bring him laud,*
> *The Babe, the Son of Mary.*
>
> —William C. Dix

Pilgrimage

He was six months old and certainly the handsomest baby ever been born to mortal humans. Despite the fact that his dad was a pointy-headed, narrow-shouldered, long-legged version of an intercontinental ballistic missile, this darling was worthy of magazine covers.

And I wanted to show him off, so that Christmas we loaded our 1979 Honda Civic, a car so small we parked it in a shoebox at night, and started our pilgrimage to California, home of the Wilcox dynasty.

We learned early in the trip that two new parents could not pack enough swaddling clothes for a major producer of "landfill."

We also learned that a woman traveling at 60 miles an hour leaning over the back of her seat to re-swaddle a dirty infant could become a bit tense at sharp turns.

But perhaps the biggest lesson we learned on our journey from Oklahoma to the Promised Land was that those teething cookies doctors recommend can turn a fairly well-kept interior into a dough-covered page from Dante's *Inferno*. Never has so much cookie spit been created by so little of an angel as was produced during those 1,800 miles.

Not even a full box of wipes seemed sufficient against such a monumental task.

Needless to say, this trio of travelers was quite

glad to see the front door of the family home late that third night of travel. So we cleaned our little Benjamin up as well as we could, put him in his little Moses basket, placed him at the front door, rang the doorbell, and ran.

We could hear the screams all the way down the Christmas-lit block.

GUIDANCE

Few kids make it through the holidays, much less their childhood, without hearing this dreaded threat from a frustrated mother or babysitter.

. . . just as the last drop of hot grape cider spills onto the brand-new white carpet;

. . . just as the last snip of the scissors reduces the Christmas wreath to a naked halo;

. . . just as the laundry detergent turns the dishwasher into Mt. St. Helens;

. . . just as the last box of Jell-O is emptied into the fishbowl;

. . . just as the red paint begins to dry on the snowy front yard—

"You just wait until your father gets home!"

Fathers across America have traditionally been the bearers of bad tidings as soon as they leave the corporate world of the highway and enter the much larger world of child-hoodlums and adolescent felons on Sunny Lane.

It's almost as if the "D" in "Dad" stands for "discipline."

Wouldn't it be interesting if this perceived forecast of doom were more like the announcement of the arrival of Santa Claus? Instead of making dads the bad guys, they could be the fantasy heroes they've always wanted to be.

"Just wait until your dad gets home—then you

can go to the North Pole on your cardboard sleigh"
or

"Just wait until your dad gets home—then he'll
go buy you a new toboggan" or

"Just wait until your dad gets home—then
jump on the bed in your parka and snow boots until your head pops through the ceiling."

Discipline is not punishment only. Discipline is
also praise.

For every spanking in a child's life, there ought
to be 100 strokes of "Atta girl—I knew you could
do it!"

For every "You've been a bad boy," there needs
to be 1,000 times of "Wow, kid! You're the greatest!"

Discipline is guidance, and nothing draws followers like praise.

Just as the great star in the sky guided the wise
men to the cradle of Christ, let our discipline guide
our children to His cross.

Visitors

The birth of Jesus brought many visitors: magi, shepherds, and angels. Mary and Joseph were far too preoccupied to worry about picking up the place, preparing casseroles, or making a good first impression, however.

No, those are the trappings of our visiting rituals today, and during the Christmas season especially, nothing thrills us quite like the anticipation of seeing family and friends for the holidays.

My favorite childhood memories of Christmas center around the tree and seeing Aunt Billie and Uncle Herb's 1962 Chevrolet station wagon pulling up to the curb out front early Christmas morning. (I must tell you the truth right here, right now: those two dear people still drive that same car as if it were brand new off the lot. Amazing what a little tender loving care does for a piece of machinery like that.)

The sight of my aunt and uncle meant, of course, that our tickle partner, cousin Gail, was not far behind. How we used to love to pin one another to the floor and tickle each other's ribs until tears of hysteria flowed and we would lie flat on the carpet panting for breath.

Christmas was the only day of the year that fudge, peanut brittle, and Mom's divine divinity were served for breakfast as we dove, sometimes headfirst, into the collage of red-and-green paper, gold-and-white bows, boxes, bags, and stockings.

When the gifts had been opened—slowly at our house, one at a time with lots of time given to admiration and gratitude—and Andy Williams had piped his final strains of "Winter Wonderland," we headed to the feast of turkey and dressing, stories and gossip, laughter and wonder.

It was almost always an emotional letdown when the sun began to set and our relatives began to pack up their station wagon for the half-hour drive home. Tickling gave way to "Gotcha last!" and Billie, who has never, ever thrown anything away, grabbed her bag of paper and ribbons for next year, and Herb went to the bathroom "one last time." It all seemed to end as fast as it came.

But then the next day, who should pop over but Grandma and Grandpa, Aunt Aleene and Uncle Wendell, and cousin Kenny with his pompadour and skin-tight blue jeans. That Kenny was a rebel without a cause and the idol of this little squirt and his twin little squirt.

Who knew whom tomorrow might bring, ringing the front doorbell?

SECRETS

Matthew records that Mary kept many of her emotions locked away in her heart, secreted from the rest of the world, far too meaningful to share with anyone.

As children, most of us have sworn ourselves to secrecy at least once or twice, haven't we? Maybe it was the secret that your best friend, Joey, was in love with that cute second-grade girl in Miss Brown's class—the one with the pigtails and bobby socks.

Or perhaps it was the secret that our brother had sneaked a box of Jell-O, sweet-flavored powder in beautifully sealed wax paper, to his room for an after-school snack. (Little did he know that his own devices would reveal his pilfering when he opened his mouth and showed his lime-green tongue at dinner.)

Or maybe it was the hidden story of the broken promise, or the lost set of Dad's tools, or the poem we wrote our mom for Mothers' Day.

At times in our lives, what we're thinking or what we're doing or whom we love seems too important to tell to anyone.

What was it that Mary kept locked away from the people around her? Maybe we'll never know . . . or perhaps we know already what it was.

Escape

That first step is the hard one!

Whether it's taken during the altar call of a church service, down the aisle at your wedding, or toward the end of the high dive at the local YMCA, the initial move is the hardest move of all.

Several years ago, Jerry had had a rough year with his new boss, who had come in and had immediately begun making some huge changes—restructuring, firing, reassigning, renaming, and the list went on. Some of Jerry's colleagues had been caught in the crosshairs, and frankly, Jerry was still angry.

Has that ever happened to you?

One night at a restaurant when Jerry and his wife were with some friends, the conversation turned to his work. Before long they were all venting their frustrations, sometimes rather vigorously, feeling better with every stab at the boss's back. Soon they were even laughing at the man.

Imagine their shock when a lady from a nearby table who was walking away said, "I've never heard people say such awful things about another person."

That certainly put a damper on the evening. Jerry was instantly afraid that this woman would call his boss first thing Monday morning and he would be the next to go. It was humiliating—but the humbling (and healing) would come later.

Months went by, and nothing ever happened to Jerry at work, so his fears began to subside. At the end of the fiscal year, his boss announced his retirement. But Jerry had never forgotten what he said about his boss and what that woman at the restaurant said to him.

Just days before the boss was to leave the company, Jerry apologized for talking behind his back. The boss was honestly surprised and completely gracious, telling Jerry that he had nothing but good feelings for him.

The relationship was healed.

The best way to escape the clutches of evil is to take the first step away from it and a second step toward the safe harbor of grace and good.

For Joseph and Mary, the escape into Egypt was the first step away from Herod and his reign of terror. It was not easy for them to walk away from home, but as we must recognize, our haven of rest is often in that first step toward reconciliation.

Wouldn't the holidays be the perfect time to escape the evil of gossip and backstabbing and take the first step toward God's peace and understanding?

INCENSED, FRANKNESS, AND MIRTH

On one of those typically warm, lingering summer evenings in California 27 years ago, much like the other 364 days of the year, four young men with little to do went Christmas caroling. I was one of them.

We were terribly young, as I reflect—impetuous, spontaneous, and nearly insane—but we did have, at least, the decency to drive to a faraway neighborhood to preserve the integrity of our parents and all they had worked for.

Our motive was simple and twofold: first, we sought to amuse a few strangers in a time when fun was piteously lacking in North America; and second, we had to have some bumbleberry pie.

Bumbleberry pie, to the four of us, was more than a dessert, more than a slice of oozing fruit and juices, more than a palatable pleasure dome. To us, bumbleberry pie was a way of life, and on this night, dressed in ragged T-shirts, cutoffs, and San Francisco Giants ball caps, we had to have some of that pie.

The trouble was, we had no money.

The first house we approached had its sizable front door closed and its brass-plated porch light extinguished. We could see through the windows that someone was home, so we joined our voices on the front lawn and began to sing in one-part harmony: "Joy to the world! the Lord is come; / Let earth receive her King."

After six verses, some of which we created as we sang, the door finally opened, and we cheerfully greeted the 60-something couple.

"Good evening," we said. "We're four college students raising money, and we'd like to sing for you."

The look on their faces was way beyond puzzlement and skepticism, but the man did finally reach into his pocket, pulled out two quarters, and handed them to us through a crack in the screen door. Then he did the unexpected—he shut the door.

Nonplussed, we went to the next house . . . and the next . . . and the next. Some of the folks ignored us. Some threw nickels at us and told us to get out. At one house we even got a whole dollar. The majority of those we visited seemed to enjoy the unseasonable friendliness of four weird teenagers dressed in ragged T-shirts, cutoffs, and ball caps.

Three hours later, we had enough change to buy our bumbleberry pie, compliments of some unsuspecting strangers. But more than that, our caroling had given us a memory that has remained with me all these years hence—and will for a lifetime.

I feel that's what caroling is all about.

The Escape

Matt. 2:12-23

But when they returned to their own land, they didn't go through Jerusalem to report to Herod, for God had warned them in a dream to go home another way.

After they were gone, an angel of the Lord appeared to Joseph in a dream. "Get up and flee to Egypt with the baby and his mother," the angel said, "and stay there until I tell you to return, for King Herod is going to try to kill the child." That same night he left for Egypt with Mary and the baby, and stayed there until King Herod's death. This fulfilled the prophet's prediction,

"I have called my Son from Egypt."

Herod was furious when he learned that the astrologers had disobeyed him. Sending soldiers to Bethlehem, he ordered them to kill every baby boy two years old and under, both in the town and on the nearby farms, for the astrologers had told him the star first appeared to them two years before.

This brutal action of Herod's fulfilled the prophecy of Jeremiah,

"Screams of anguish come from Ramah,
Weeping unrestrained;
Rachel weeping for her children,
Uncomforted—
For they are dead."

When Herod died, an angel of the Lord appeared in a dream to Joseph in Egypt, and told him, "Get up and take the baby and his mother back to Israel, for those who were trying to kill the child are dead."

So he returned immediately to Israel with Jesus and His mother. But on the way he was frightened to learn that the new king was Herod's son, Archelaus. Then, in another dream, he was warned not to go to Judea, so they went to Galilee instead, and lived in Nazareth. This fulfilled the prediction of the prophets concerning the Messiah,

"He shall be called a Nazarene" (TLB).

FURY

Nobody likes a troublemaker, except maybe another troublemaker. Just ask John Rocker. Or Dennis Rodman. Or Mike Tyson. Or King Herod.

When the leader of the land realized that the magi had failed to report to him following their visit to the newborn King of the Jews, he became furious and ordered the murder of all boys under the age of two.

Most of us pride ourselves on our abilities to hold our tempers, to count to ten. But it seems every corporate board, church board, school committee, work crew, or even just a group of friends has at least one member whose main goal every day is to stir up trouble. If the majority wants to turn left, he or she insists on going right. If 11 out of 12 say yes, he or she will be the one to say no.

And this one person always becomes furious at being the lone voice of *reason* (his or her reason, at least).

It boils down to a fragile ego that always has to be right, and we all know that the person who always *has to be right* is rarely correct. Unfortunately, such an individual is so strong willed that he or she cannot be content until the whole group is in chaos, with people yelling, arguing, or punching.

Sometimes a family will grow one of these people. When everyone else is ready to leave the house, this person screams from the bathroom that he or she is having a bad hair day. As soon as the family sits down to a succulent steak dinner, this person announces that he or she has suddenly become a vegetarian (and casually announces at the dinner table one night, "You're all murderers!").

There's a big difference between being a *change agent* and being a *troublemaker*, and it all lies in motive.

If the motive is progress and improvement, that's leadership. But if the motive is selfishness and dissension, we've become like Herod—furious and vengeful.

A Two-Year-Old's Secret Stocking

Sociologists say that one defining characteristic of a family is its traditions, those repeated activities and rituals that move from mere routine to the deep tissue of the heart.

When I was growing up in California, one of our many Christmas traditions involved our Christmas stockings, hanging from the hearth above the fireplace. My mom had made them for us three kids with each name at the top—Judi, Jimmy, and Johnny.

As the season progressed, they became lumpier and lumpier with each surprise and treasure that mysteriously appeared inside. (We thought Santa visited every night at our house.) With each lump, our eyes got bigger and our hearts lighter.

This was the season of wonder.

On Christmas Eve, after all the activities of church and friends ended, we were finally allowed to open our stockings, signaling the beginning of gift-opening that would last throughout most of the next day.

I don't remember many of the gifts that were inside, but I do remember that every year we got a book of LifeSavers and a giant peppermint stick the size of my skinny arm.

To this day, I hang that same stocking on our stairway banister, along with stockings for my wife, our two sons, and one daughter-in-law, thereby passing on the tradition of my childhood.

The truth of the matter is that I still get rather excited on Christmas Eve.

THE CHRISTMAS TREE

It was always a Saturday,
   sometime between lunch and dusk,
   but closer to dusk.
   Mornings were too filled with chores,
      painting the potty with Pine Sol,
      "Pledging" the dust off coffee tables,
      riding the "Tide-al" wave of laundry back into
         the drawers.

The Christmas lights had been woven onto their nails,
   which were annually left on the eaves for ease,
      if you please,
   the Saturday before,
      and now it was time to get
         the tree.
   Douglas fir? Scotch pine?
   As long as it was tall,
         and full,
         and fresh, it didn't matter.

We slipped into our warmest coats and shoes,
   two pairs of socks, thank you,
      for the drive and climb up nearby Mt. Hamilton to
         find the tree.
   A family effort, it took both parents to wield the
      pickaxe on the tree—

Mom did the picking,
Dad the axing.
    Once home, the tree belonged to Dad,
        and Hoover, for we always flocked it
        white as mock snow.

(The instant snowstorm, spewing from the vacuum
    hose, fascinated us boys—
    "Why not the whole yard, Dad?")

The tree had to be white for the color wheel, and
    as soon as it was dark, usually after dinner,
    we'd dash outside to see
        Green . . . turquoise . . . blue . . .
           "Ahhhhhhh!"
        Violet . . . red . . . orange . . .
           "Ooooooooo!"
        Yellow . . . lemonlime . . . green, again . . .
           "Ohhhhhhh!"

Of all the homes in all the neighborhoods of my child-
    hood,
    ours was the most beautiful,
        the most exciting,
        the warmest
    because the tree in the middle of the picture win-
        dow
        had been a family effort.
And we were a real Christmas family.

KNEELING

The 10-year-old came to the breakfast table after a night of peaceful slumber, despite a Christmas snowstorm that had blanketed the neighborhood in 12 inches of frozen white and had brought the little burgh to a virtual standstill.

"How'd you sleep last night?" his mother asked him as she poured hot maple syrup over his waffles.

Still only semiconscious and unable to articulate real words, all he could muster this dark morning was a monosyllabic "ugh."

And then one of those thought bubbles that were constantly floating around in the little boy's brain and would occasionally dislodge at odd moments spontaneously burst and tumbled out of his mouth into his mother's heart.

"You know," he said, "on the nights when you come tuck me in at night, Mom, I don't have any bad dreams. But when you forget to, I dream bad things and hear bad things all night."

His mother laid down her cup of coffee and put her hand on his baby-smooth arm. In the tone of love that's unique to mothers all over the world, she smiled and said, "Oh, I come in to tuck you in every night, Honey—even when you've already fallen asleep. And I kneel by your bed and whisper a prayer for sweet dreams."

And the habit of a praying mother was revealed.

Long after we've been weaned and potty-trained, fed and taught to drive, raised and educated, and are gone with kids of our own, our mothers still enter the rooms of our souls, the secret places of our hearts, to kneel by our beds at night, tuck us in, and whisper the snowstorms away.

FLEEING IN FEAR

Bill was chased all the way to first grade one day before Christmas break by a big, black dog. Next to going to the dentist's office, this was the most frightening experience of his childhood years—even more than being called to the principal's office in third grade, more than breaking his violin bow in fourth grade, more than Doug Dergwagen's threat in fifth grade.

Today Bill is a middle-aged businessman with two grown children, but every time his wife asks him to go for a walk with her, he again becomes a six-year-old bundle of nerves, looking for any excuse to stay within the safety of his suburban fortress.

He is convinced that all unleashed dogs are killers, no matter the size or demeanor, the time of day, or the time of the year. He sees large dogs with the same eyes with which the residents of Amity Island viewed a great white shark—with giant, human-eating jaws. And small dogs are little less than landlocked piranha, Bill says, chomping for the chance to gnaw on middle-aged ankles.

This is just about the same kind of fear we read about in Matthew's account when he talks about Mary, Joseph, and the little baby Jesus packing up their humble belongings and fleeing into Egypt to avoid the murderous wrath of King Herod.

That kind of fear numbs the senses and pushes the adrenaline through the veins at unprecedented speed.

But during this frightening flight, an angel spoke to the new little family on muleback and protected their spirits as well as their very beings.

Praise the Child of Christmas, who dwells within us and brings the comfort and sanctuary of angels' wings.

> *Angels we have heard on high,*
> *Sweetly singing o'er the plains,*
> *And the mountains in reply,*
> *Echoing their joyous strains.*
> *Gloria in excelsis Deo!*
> *Gloria in excelsis Deo!*

Exile

Anyone who saw Steve Martin when he was a stand-up comedian will never forget the moment he proclaimed to a stunned and hysterical audience—as his legs and feet flailed in every direction possible—"Look—I've got happy feet!"

Sometimes we, too, get happy feet when it comes to impulsive behavior. You and I know all too well what "impulsive" means, especially when it comes to Christmas shopping.

Impulse forces us to buy that compass/nail clipper/radio/flashlight combination gizmo at the checkout counter of our local grocery store to put under Uncle Henry's Christmas tree. Impulse is the force that makes us buy two blouses for ourselves for every blouse we get as a Christmas gift. It's the inability to say no to the "death by chocolate" dessert our hostess serves after our 8,000-calorie Christmas dinner.

Exile is banishment from home; sometimes it's enforced by others, but often it's self-imposed.

Jake had just gone to the university for his first taste of freedom from the restrictions of home when he met Jeffrey, the local "party animal." By Christmas break, Jake was drinking several six-packs every weekend and experimenting with harder drugs.

As the holidays neared, he was stealing from friends and acquaintances in the fraternity house and from the register at work in order to keep himself high and low, whatever the situation called for.

Jake had gotten "happy feet" that he could no longer control. He was in a self-inflicted exile from the Christian home in which he had been nurtured and loved. His "happy feet" were taking him in every direction possible toward sin, crime, and certain harm. And in the process, he was destroying everything he knew to be sacred.

The greatest sign of maturity—spiritual, psychological and otherwise—is our ability to discern where our feet should go. Have we exiled ourselves from the life we were intended to have through the birth and resurrection of Christ?

Or are we waking up each morning this Christmas season, searching for the footprints of the Messiah to lead us ever closer to our heavenly home?

THE CHRISTMAS MORNING HUB

Bright yellow, like the sun that
    sprayed through the window over the sink,
    and just as warm—
especially on Christmas Saturdays
    when Mom fixed
    her lemon meringue pies
    and pecan pies
    and pumpkin pies
    that always left crust enough
    for cinnamon swirls,
    sprinkled with sugar—
        and the Christmas divinity
        and chocolate fudge.
Our kitchen was at the center
    of our home,
the center of the universe.
    Bordered in wrought-iron trivets,
    auburn cupboards
    (that hid the Christmas-colored Trix),
    and rich echoes of day-tales;
It was the room that pulsed with
    the beat of our family.
The kitchen was not without its own
    routine, though—it was, after all,
        a Wilcox, too—
manufacturing cereal and eggs every other day,

broken only by
> *Saturday's pancakes, waffles, and French toast,*
and Sunday's sweet rolls.

On Christmas morning,
> *the hub became Mrs. Santa's buffet—*
> *from her pies*
>> *to her ham*
>> *to her yams*
>> *to the turkey*
>>> *and dressing*
>>> *and cranberries*
>>> *and rolls.*
A daylong feast and a lifetime memory.

As the wheel revolves around a hub,
> *so our family five*
>> *and my many memories*
> *of home*
revolve around our yellow kitchen
> *on a red-and-green Christmas morn.*